W9-DIU-202

TOUGH GUIDES

HOW TO SURVIVE IN THE
OCEAN

LOUISE SPILSBURY

PowerKiDS press.

New York

Published in 2013 by The Rosen Publishing Group, Inc.
29 East 21st Street, New York, NY 10010

Copyright © 2013 by The Rosen Publishing Group, Inc.

All rights reserved. No part of this book may be reproduced in any form without permission in writing from the publisher, except by a reviewer.

Produced for Rosen by Calcium Creative Ltd
Editors for Calcium Creative Ltd: Sarah Eason and Jennifer Sanderson
US Editor: Sara Antill
Designer: Simon Borrough

Photo credits: Cover: Shutterstock: Keren-seg, Willyam Bradberry. Inside: Dreamstime: Cornelius20 10l, 22l, Matthew Trommer 21t; Shutterstock: Rich Carey 6l, 18l, Cbpix 18c, Clearviewstock 17c, Djgis 11c, Undersea Discoveries 19t, Tom Dowd 12cr, Elena Elisseeva 10c, Idreamphoto 14c, Chaikovskiy Igor 6c, Irabel8 20c, Andrew Jalbert 4c, Juhana Lampinen 22cr, Iakov Kalinin 4l, 16l, 28l, DJ Mattaar 13t, William Attard McCarthy 7t, PhotoHappiness 4tr, Jason Patrick Ross 27cl, Lisa S. 16c, Keren-seg 14l, 26l, Galushko Sergey 12l, 24l, Shotgun 24c, AntonSokolov 8cl, Kayros Studio 8br, Tandemich 8l, 20l, Guido Vrola 9c, Wonderisland 5tl, Worldswildlifewonders 15t; US Coastguard: Petty Officer 3rd Class Brandyn Hill 23c, U.S. Army photo by Arthur McQueen 28cl; US Navy: Mass Communication Specialist 3rd Class Heidi McCormick 29tl, Mass Communication Specialist 2nd Class Bryan Weyers 25t.

Library of Congress Cataloging-in-Publication Data

Spilsbury, Louise.
 How to survive in the ocean / by Louise Spilsbury.
     p. cm. — (Tough guides)
 Includes index.
 ISBN 978-1-4488-7868-0 (library binding) — ISBN 978-1-4488-7933-5 (pbk.) —
 ISBN 978-1-4488-7939-7 (6-pack)
 1. Wilderness survival—Juvenile literature. 2. Survival at sea—Juvenile literature. I. Title.
 GV200.5.S65 2013
 613.69—dc23

                                2011051882

Manufactured in the United States of America

CPSIA Compliance Information: Batch #SW12PK: For Further Information contact Rosen Publishing, New York, New York at 1-800-237-9932

CONTENTS

SURVIVAL! 4

A SINKING SHIP 6

STAYING AFLOAT 8

SALTY WATER 10

CATCHING FISH 12

CATCHING SEAFOOD 14

FINDING YOUR WAY 16

SHARK ATTACK! 18

STORMS AT SEA 20

TOO HOT, TOO COLD 22

PIRATES! 24

STRANDED 26

RESCUED! 28

GLOSSARY 30

FURTHER READING 31

WEBSITES 31

INDEX 32

DEC 3 2012

SURVIVAL!

We live on a blue planet. About 70 percent of Earth's surface is covered by oceans. Every day thousands of people work on the ocean, travel across it, or visit it to go sailing, diving, fishing, and swimming. The ocean is wild and beautiful, but it can also be one of the most dangerous and challenging places on Earth.

shipwreck

SHIPWRECKS
WHAT: sunken ships on the ocean floor
HOW MANY: more than 3 million worldwide

Moken person

Fierce storms can send huge waves crashing into a boat and even sink it. To survive on the ocean, people have to stay afloat, keep warm, find water and food, and escape the hungry jaws of ocean monsters, such as the great white shark! How do people survive when they come face to face with these dangers?

TOUGH TIP

Watch out for oceanic whitetip sharks. Food is scarce for these hunters, so they make a meal of whatever they can find, including ship and airplane disaster victims.

MOKEN PEOPLE

WHAT: the Moken dive for fish off islands in Myanmar and Thailand
HOW: Moken people see twice as well underwater as other people!

A SINKING SHIP

If a ship starts to sink, it is vital to stay calm. People who panic make mistakes, so take a few deep breaths and get to the ship's deck as quickly as you can. Send out a **Mayday**, which is a radio message to say you are in trouble and you need help. Make sure you say who you are and where you are as clearly as you can.

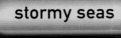
stormy seas

STORMS AT SEA
WHAT: on average two large ships sink worldwide every week
HOW: most shipwrecks are caused by storms

sinking boat

If you must **abandon** the ship, find a **life jacket** and put it on. Collect some emergency items for the life raft, such as food, water, and a first aid kit. Load these into the life raft carefully and quickly, and make sure you escape before the ship goes down!

TOUGH TIP

Some people say ships do not suck people down with them when they sink, but survivors who have escaped sinking ships say it does happen. Do not take chances. Move away from a sinking ship quickly.

SINKING SHIPS
WHAT: sinking ships often roll onto one side as they sink
ACTION: watch out for objects sliding around and hold onto the sides of the ship to avoid slipping

The biggest risk in the ocean is **drowning**. If you are not in a life raft it is vital to stay on top of the water. A simple life jacket can save your life. It helps you to float and it keeps your head above water. No life jacket? Hold onto something that is floating by, such as a log or a life ring.

life jacket

LIFE JACKET
WHAT: helps to keep you afloat
HOW: life jackets are filled with a very light material, such as foam

8

TOUGH TIP

When an Australian fishing boat sank in just 30 seconds, the three fishermen inside had no time to get into a life raft. They were lucky. An ice box from the sinking ship floated to the surface so they clung to it until a rescue helicopter found and rescued them.

Swimming is hard work, so if you do not have a life jacket, float on your back with your arms and legs spread out. This will keep your face out of the water and you may even be able to sleep for short periods of time.

life ring

LIFE RING
WHAT: can keep you afloat and help others rescue you
HOW: many are attached to rope that is used to pull people to safety

SALTY WATER

N o human can survive without water for more than three days, but you should never drink seawater. The salt in seawater can make you ill and even kill you. To survive you need to catch rainwater in your hands or any container you can find. You can also use a T-shirt or sail to catch this life-giving freshwater.

catching rainwater

WATER
FACT: two-thirds of the human body by weight is made of water
THREAT: you need to drink 8 pints (2 liters) of water a day

This expert survival tip turns seawater into drinking water. Put seawater into a container and stand it in an empty cup. Wrap clear plastic over the top so that heat from the Sun **evaporates** some of the seawater. When **water vapor condenses** on the plastic, it leaves the salt behind and freshwater drips into the cup.

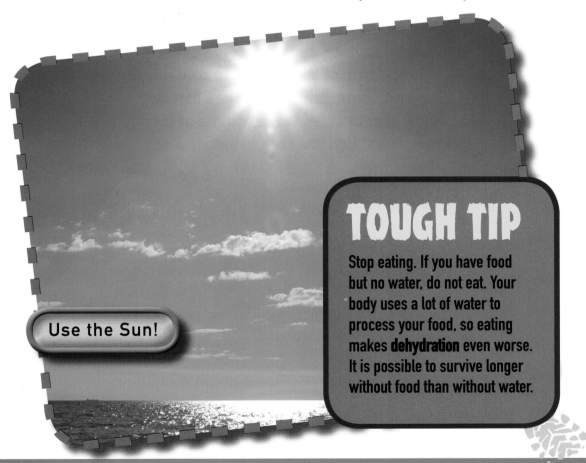

Use the Sun!

TOUGH TIP

Stop eating. If you have food but no water, do not eat. Your body uses a lot of water to process your food, so eating makes **dehydration** even worse. It is possible to survive longer without food than without water.

SALTWATER
PROBLEM: seawater is too salty to drink
ACTION: when sunlight evaporates seawater, the salt is left behind

CATCHING FISH

The ocean is full of fish that provide food for many of the world's people, but be careful which ones you try to catch. The long arms of a jellyfish can give a killer sting and some fish have spikes that can poison you. Luckily, in the middle of the ocean, most fish are safe to eat.

flying fish

FLYING FISH
SIZE: grow up to 18 inches (45 cm) long
HOW TO CATCH THEM: may leap out of the water and land in boats

mackerel shoal

Use any cloth you have to make a fishing net. Hold it underwater and scoop it upward quickly to trap a fish. Bend a wire to make a fishing hook and tie it to a shoelace. Put tiny fish on the hook as **bait** to catch a larger fish.

TOUGH TIP

Out of the ocean fish go rotten quickly, so make your own dried fish snacks. Dried fish are safe to eat for several days. Remove the bones and guts as soon as you catch the fish. Then cut the fish into thin strips and hang them to dry.

MACKEREL
SIZE: grow up to 16 inches (41 cm) long
HOW TO CATCH THEM: use a strip of fish as bait

CATCHING SEAFOOD

The deep blue ocean is bursting with life and fish are not the only choice of food. Seaweed is salty and tough, but it is good to eat as long as you have lots of drinking water. Sea turtles are easy to catch because they swim to the surface every few minutes to breathe, but try to avoid eating them because they are **endangered**.

sea turtle

SEA TURTLE
SIZE: grows up to 46 inches (117 cm) long
WHAT: it is illegal to eat sea turtles in many countries because they are under threat

seaweed

All birds are safe to eat so catch any seabirds that you can. Many seabirds feed on the ocean's surface so if you stay quiet they may land close by. If one lands on your life raft you might be able to grab it, or spear it using a knife tied to an oar.

SEAWEED
WHAT: eat only living seaweed
USE: can be eaten raw or as a boiled vegetable

TOUGH TIP

Three boys lost in the Pacific Ocean survived for 50 days before they were spotted by a fishing boat. They lived on rainwater, coconuts, and a type of seabird that they caught when it landed on their boat. They killed the bird and ate it raw.

FINDING YOUR WAY

In the middle of the ocean all you can see for miles (km) around is deep blue water, so how do you find your way? In the past sailors used the position of the Sun, Moon, and stars in the sky to **navigate**, but this takes skill. At night a distant, flashing light could be a lighthouse so aim for that.

message in a bottle

MESSAGE IN A BOTTLE
WHAT: put a message in a bottle and toss it out to sea
WHY: in 2011 a ship's crew threw a message in a bottle out to sea. The message was found and they were rescued.

TOUGH TIP

Send signals to help rescuers find you. Turn a flashlight on and off if you see a boat or airplane during the night. In the daytime, use a mirror and focus the reflection of the Sun to get people's attention.

Do not miss out on the chance of rescue. Watch for signs that you are drifting close to land. Deep water is dark green-blue and shallow water is lighter, which may mean land is near. Watch birds, too. There are usually many more birds near land than over the open ocean.

the night sky

NORTH STAR

WHAT: the most important star for navigation
WHY: an imaginary line drawn from this star to the nearest point on the **horizon** shows the direction north

SHARK ATTACK!

Large, sharp-toothed sharks are the most frightening animals in the ocean. These torpedo-shaped fish have powerful tails that push them through water at high speeds. Great white sharks are the deadliest. They swim up from below and bite into **prey** with a mouthful of 300 sawlike teeth.

reef shark

REEF SHARK
SIZE: up to 6 feet (1.8 m) long
THREAT: attacks swimmers that it mistakes as prey

tiger shark

I SURVIVED

For 13-year-old Bethany Hamilton a day at the beach in Hawaii almost ended in disaster. She was surfing when a tiger shark suddenly darted up and bit off her left arm. Bethany escaped and managed to use her right arm to swim to safety, warning other surfers about the attack as she went.

If sharks see or hear something in the water they check it out, so do not kick and splash around too much. Sharks are also attracted to blood, so if you are injured try to stay out of the water. If you are attacked, kick or punch the shark in the nose and swim away!

TIGER SHARK
SIZE: grows to 25 feet (7.6 m) long, weighs more than 1,900 pounds (861 kg)
THREAT: sharp teeth and powerful jaws can kill

STORMS AT SEA

Ocean storms can be terrifying. Howling winds can tear off parts of a ship and whip up huge waves, which toss boats around like toys. Winds can also wash people off boats into the rough sea. The best way to survive a storm at sea is to avoid it. Do not set out if a storm is on the way.

huge ocean wave

MONSTER WAVE

SIZE: can be 100 feet (30 m) high; that is taller than the Lincoln Memorial

THREAT: can capsize and sink boats and ships at sea

hurricane seen from space

TOUGH TIP

If you are in a life raft when a storm hits, you should be able to ride over high waves safely. Make sure that you close the raft covers and flaps to keep out as much water as possible.

Hurricanes are the most dangerous storms of all. Hurricane winds form over warm oceans and spin around and around in a spiral at high speeds. The center, or eye, of a hurricane can be calm, but its winds can create enormous waves. Some waves can be as tall as a three-story building!

HURRICANE
WIND SPEED: up to 200 miles per hour (321 km/h)
THREAT: can damage and sink ships at sea

TOO HOT, TOO COLD

With the Sun reflecting off large areas of flat water, it can get very hot on the ocean. Skin burns quickly in the Sun on an ocean and getting too hot makes people very ill. Try to make a cover from sails or cloth to shade you from the Sun. If it is very hot, wet your clothes to keep cool.

Cover up in the sun.

SUN SAFETY
THREAT: invisible **ultraviolet rays** in sunlight burn and damage skin
ACTION: wear sunglasses and clothing to cover yourself

TOUGH TIP

If you are in the water, cold is a real danger. The best thing to do is hold your knees up to your chest with your legs crossed. This is called the HELP (Heat Escape Lessening Position) and it helps your body to hold onto its warmth for longer.

If you are stranded in a life raft on a cold ocean it is important to keep dry because being wet will make you feel colder. Cover up with blankets, huddle together with other people, or flap your arms and move your body.

HELP position

HELP
FACT: you lose about 50 percent of your body heat through your head
ACTION: use the HELP position to keep your head out of the water

PIRATES!

Long ago, fierce pirates attacked sailing ships with cannons and pistols. They used daggers and swords to frighten crews into handing over their **cargo**. Ships today are bigger, safer, and faster, but pirates are still a real danger. Pirates often attack at night and hold the crew at gunpoint while they steal money, cargo, televisions, and clothes.

skull and crossbones flag

SKULL AND CROSSBONES
IN THE PAST: used by pirates to scare people
TODAY: means something is dangerous, such as poison

24

US Navy captures modern-day pirates

TOUGH TIP

In 2005 Jay Barry and his partner were on a trip around the world when they were attacked by armed pirates. When Barry saw four pirates speeding toward him, he rammed his ship at full speed into their boat. The shocked pirates turned and left, and Barry lived to tell the tale!

Today some pirates steal people, too. They **kidnap** people from their boats and hold them to **ransom** for large sums of money. The best way to survive a pirate attack is never to get into it. Before you travel on the ocean, find out if the area is safe.

MODERN-DAY PIRATES

WHAT: pirates from Somalia **hijacked** 35 ships

WHEN: the first nine months of 2010

STRANDED

Ocean dangers do not end when survivors reach an island. People can be injured or killed when boats hit jagged rocks or **coral reefs** near shore, so try to land on sandy beaches when waves are gentle. Once ashore, your first job is to find water. If there is no stream, collect coconuts as they contain lots of freshwater and fill you up, too.

desert island

DESERT ISLAND
WHAT: coconut trees grow on many desert island shores
HOW: coconuts float across oceans and wash up on islands where they grow into trees

You will also need to build a shelter. A roof of branches and leaves protects you from the Sun and rain. You could use wood or the life raft as a floor to keep you off the ground and away from deadly scorpions and snakes!

TOUGH TIP

Build a fire. You can use a fire to cook fish, boil water, keep you warm, and it can help you get rescued! Keep piles of wood nearby so you can light them quickly, to act as a signal when you see an airplane or ship.

fire signal

FIRE SIGNAL
WHAT: the best way to signal for help in the dark
HOW: build three fires in a triangle. This is an international distress signal.

RESCUED!

It is a real challenge to survive on the ocean. If you know how to find food and water and keep safe, you could stay alive until a rescue boat finds you. This can take a long time, so keep cheerful by singing, telling stories, and making plans for the future.

helicopter rescue

RESCUE HELICOPTER
SIZE: about 70 feet (21 m) long
ACTION: lowers a cable to lift people out of the water

lifted to safety

I SURVIVED

Some people do not believe their remarkable story, but three Mexican fishermen claim to have survived at sea for a record-breaking 289 days in a wind-wrecked fishing boat. They say they sang songs, danced, and played air guitar to keep busy, and drank rainwater and ate raw fish and seabirds to survive.

Being rescued is the final challenge. Rescue is difficult and dangerous in rough ocean waves. Helicopters drop rescue swimmers into the ocean who battle through strong seas to reach survivors. Survivors are lifted to safety on a long cable that dangles from the helicopter high above the stormy seas.

RESCUE SWIMMER
PROBLEM: lifting an injured person to safety
ACTION: rescue swimmer lifts the victim in a lift strap that goes under his or her arms

GLOSSARY

abandon (uh-BAN-dun) To leave a thing or place.

bait (BAYT) Food put on a hook or in a net to attract and catch fish.

capsize (KAP-syz) To turn over in the water.

cargo (KAHR-goh) The things carried by a ship or plane.

condenses (kun-DENTS-es) Changes from a gas into a liquid.

coral reefs (KOR-ul REEFS) Rock-like structures built by tiny ocean animals.

dehydration (dee-hy-DRAY-shen) Illness caused by lack of drinking water.

drowning (DROWN-ing) Dying underwater because you cannot breathe.

endangered (in-DAYN-jerd) Describes a type of animal that soon may no longer exist.

evaporates (ih-VA-puh-rayts) Changes from a liquid into a gas.

hijacked (HY-jakd) Stopped and stolen a boat.

horizon (huh-RY-zun) The line where the sky meets the land or the sea.

hurricanes (HUR-ih-kaynz) Violent storms with very strong, very fast spinning winds.

kidnap (KID-nap) To hold someone against their will.

life jacket (LYF JA-ket) A jacket that fills with air to help you float on water.

Mayday (MAY-day) The radio signal for help used by ships and planes all over the world.

navigate (NA-vuh-gayt) To find one's way around.

prey (PRAY) An animal that is hunted and eaten by other animals.

ransom (RAN-sum) Money paid to free a kidnapped person.

ultraviolet rays (ul-truh-VY-uh-let RAYZ) Rays given off by the Sun that can hurt your skin and eyes.

water vapor (WAH-ter VAY-pur) Water in a gas form.

FURTHER READING

Hodge, Susie. *Ocean Survival.* Extreme Habitats. New York: Gareth Stevens, 2008.

Jackson, Tom. *Inside the Mind of a Killer Shark.* Animal Instincts. New York: PowerKids Press, 2012.

Rizzo, Johnna. *Oceans: Dolphins, Sharks, Penguins, and More!.* Washington D.C.: National Geographic, 2010.

WEBSITES

Due to the changing nature of Internet links, PowerKids Press has developed an online list of websites related to the subject of this book. This site is updated regularly. Please use this link to access the list: www.powerkidslinks.com/guide/ocean/

INDEX

C
cargo, 24
coconuts, 15, 26
condensation, 11
coral reefs, 26
D
dehydration, 11
drowning, 8
E
evaporation, 11
F
fire, 14, 27
first aid, 7
fish, 12–14, 18, 27, 29
H
helicopters, 28–29
hurricane, 21
I
island, 5, 26–27
J
jellyfish, 12

L
life jacket, 7–8, 23
life raft, 7–9, 15, 21, 27
life ring, 8–9
M
Mayday, 6
N
navigation, 16–17
P
pirates, 24–25
S
scorpions, 27
sea turtles, 14
seaweed, 14–15
sharks, 5, 18–19, 31
signals, 17, 27
snakes, 27
storms, 5–6, 20–21
sunburn, 22
W
water vapor, 11